SHARK ATTACK

Tom Jackson

🌱 Crabtree Publishing Company

www.crabtreebooks.com

Crabtree Publishing Company
PMB 16A,
350 Fifth Avenue,
Suite 3308
New York, NY 10118

616 Welland Avenue,
St. Catharines, Ontario
L2M 5V6

Content development by
Shakespeare Squared

www.ShakespeareSquared.com

Published by Crabtree
Publishing Company © 2008

First published in Great Britain
in 2008 by ticktock Media Ltd,
2 Orchard Business Centre,
North Farm Road,
Tunbridge Wells, Kent, TN2 3XF

ticktock project editor:
Ruth Owen
ticktock project designer:
Sara Greasley
ticktock picture researcher:
Lizzie Knowles

With thanks to: Series Editors Honor Head and
Jean Coppendale and Consultant, Sally Morgan

Kurt Amsler / Ardea: 20. Bettmann / Corbis: 18 inset.
Brandoon Cole / www.brandoncole.com: 8t, 16, 22-23.
Brandon Cole Marine Photography / Alamy: 1. Chris and
Monique Fallows / Apex Images Cc / Oxford Scientific:
14-15. David Fleetham / Alamy: 24b. Stephen Frink /
Getty Images: 12. Ralf Kiefner / Ardea: 4-5. Natural
Geographic: 24t. Newspix / News Ltd / 3rd party
managed reproduction and supply rights: 6. Mike Parry /
Minden Pictures / FLPA: 8b. Powerstock / SuperStock:
OFC. Jeffrey L. Rotman / Corbis: 26-27b, 27 inset, 28, 29.
Sharkshield: 25t, 25b. Shutterstock: 2, 7t, 21 all, 22 inset,
24-25 background. Sipa Press/ Rex Features: 11. Southwest
News Service / Rex Features: 7b. Superstock / Shutterstock
composite: 18-19. Visual and Written SL / Alamy: 17.
Stuart Westmorland / Getty Images: 9.

Every effort has been made to trace copyright holders, and we
apologize in advance for any omissions. We would be pleased
to insert the appropriate acknowledgments in any subsequent
edition of this publication.

Library and Archives Canada Cataloguing in Publication

Jackson, Tom, 1972-
    Shark attack / Tom Jackson.

(Crabtree contact)
Includes index.
ISBN 978-0-7787-3765-0 (bound).
--ISBN 978-0-7787-3787-2 (pbk.)

    1. Shark attacks--Juvenile literature. I. Title. II. Series.

QL638.93.J33 2008   j597.3   C2008-901209-7

Library of Congress Cataloging-in-Publication Data
Jackson, Tom, 1972-
    Shark attack / Tom Jackson.
        p. cm. -- (Crabtree contact)
    Includes index.
        ISBN-13: 978-0-7787-3787-2 (pbk. : alk. paper)
        ISBN-10: 0-7787-3787-X (pbk. : alk. paper)
        ISBN-13: 978-0-7787-3765-0 (reinforced library binding : alk.
paper)
        ISBN-10: 0-7787-3765-9 (reinforced library binding : alk. paper)
    1. Shark attacks--Juvenile literature. I. Title. II. Series.

QL638.93.J33 2008
597.3--dc22

                                                    2008006261

CONTENTS

KILLER SHARK

What would **YOU** do if you got this close
to a killer shark?

Some people have lived
to tell the tale...

SHARK ATTACK!

Eric Nerhus is an Australian diver. One day, he was collecting shellfish in the ocean. The next thing Eric knew, his head was inside the mouth of a giant shark!

Eric says, "I felt the teeth dragging across my body."

Eric fought back. He poked his fingers into the shark's eye. The shark then opened its mouth, and Eric squirmed free.

Eric **stabbed** the shark with his knife. The shark swam away.

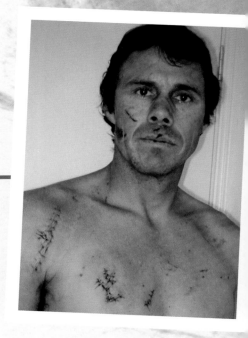

An eyewitness who saw Eric's shark attack said, "The shark was swallowing his head!"

Surfing star Bethany Hamilton lost her arm in a shark attack. She was attacked by a tiger shark while surfing in Hawaii.

Bethany didn't let the terrible experience stop her. She starting surfing again less than three months after the attack.

FOUR DAYS IN THE WATER

The crew of the warship *USS Indianapolis* were unlucky.

During World War II, *USS Indianapolis* was **torpedoed** by an enemy submarine. The ship quickly sank! Then, the sailors became the **victims** of the largest shark attack in history.

When the ship sank, 880 men were left floating helplessly in the sea. Many of them were injured and bleeding.

The blood attracted hundreds of sharks. The sharks began to attack the sailors.

Survivors say that there were hundreds of sharks swimming just below their dangling feet.
The men waited in the shark-infested water for four and a half days.

When help finally came...

...only 317 men were still alive.

THE KILLERS

There are over 330 different **species** of shark. Only 25 are known to attack humans. The main ones are:

BULL SHARK
Length – up to 11.5 feet (3.5 meters)
Weight – up to 500 pounds (230 kilograms)

TIGER SHARK
Length – up to 14 feet (4.25 meters)
Weight – up to 1,400 pounds (635 kilograms)

GREAT WHITE SHARK
Length – up to 20 feet
(6 meters)
Weight – up to 5,000
pounds (2,268 kilograms)

TASTE AND SPIT!

Great white sharks eat seals and sea lions. These animals have a lot of fat on their bodies.

Before eating its **prey**, the shark bumps it with its snout. It does this to check how much fat the prey has on its body.

The shark may also take a small bite from its prey to taste it.

A hard, bony human will not taste right to a shark.

Great white sharks that attack people have made a mistake.

They usually spit people out.
This habit is called **taste and spit.**

A **taste and spit** attack!

THE SMELL OF BLOOD

A great white shark can **detect** prey from more than a mile (1.6 kilometers) away.

First the shark heads for the sounds of splashing. Soon it can smell its prey.

A third of a shark's brain collects information about smells in the water.

The smell it detects best is blood.

Watch Out!

If you are bleeding, stay out of the water!

Sharks have an excellent sense of smell. Many types of shark can smell a single drop of blood in a million drops of water.

BREACH ATTACK!

The largest great white sharks attack their prey from below. Great whites grab their prey as they burst out of the water.

The shark sees the shape of a seal at the surface. The shark swims upward at **high speed** with its mouth open wide. The shark bursts into the air with the seal in its mouth.

Sometimes the shark swallows the seal in one gulp as it crashes back into the water.

This is called a **breach** attack.

FEEDING FRENZY!

When one shark makes a kill, the blood and splashing attracts more sharks!

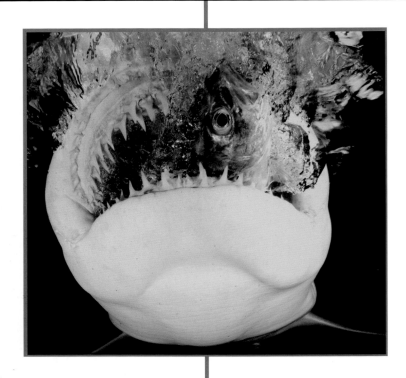

Soon a crowd of sharks gathers. The sharks kill prey as fast as possible.

They feed in a **frenzy**.

Sometimes in the frenzy, sharks attack each other. Some might even take a bite out of their own tails!

Sometimes thousands of sharks gather in a feeding frenzy.

EATING ANYTHING

When fishermen catch sharks, they get to see what is in the sharks' stomachs.

Sharks have been caught with…

…coats, shoes, deer antlers, and even a jar of nails.

One shark had eaten a chicken house!

Some scientists think that large sharks swallow these things to make themselves heavier. This makes it easier for them to dive underwater.

ANTI-ATTACK TIPS

Shark attacks are very rare,
but just in case:

- DON'T swim in the ocean at dawn or at night.

- DON'T wear sparkling jewelry in the water.

- DON'T swim near fishing boats—the bait and the blood from the fishermen's catch might attract sharks.

- If you get attacked, FIGHT BACK! Try punching the shark on the nose.

Look out for warning signs.

TECHNOLOGY

There are some clever inventions to STOP shark attacks.

Some beaches hang **shark nets** out at sea. The nets stop sharks from swimming too close to the shore.

Scientists wear **chainmail suits** when studying sharks. Sharks can't bite through these metal suits.

Chainmail suit

Surfers, swimmers, and divers can wear a small machine strapped to one of their legs. The machine gives out electrical **pulses** that scare sharks away.

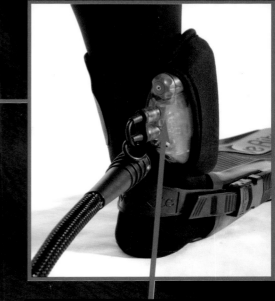

Protective oceanic device

All living things give off small electrical charges. Sharks have special parts on their heads that sense these charges. They follow the charges to find prey. A protective oceanic device gives off strong electrical pulses that sharks find unpleasant. The pulses keep sharks away without hurting them.

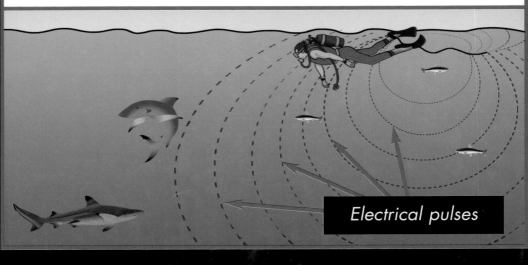

Electrical pulses

EYE-TO-EYE

Swimming with sharks is big tourist business.

Divers are dropped into shark-infested water inside a steel cage.

A large shark is strong enough to break through the bars of the cage if it wanted to.

However, after a quick taste of the cold metal bars, the shark will leave the cage alone.

Shark cages are also used by scientists. They can attach a **tracking device** to a shark from the safety of the cage.

Scientists track the sharks to find out how deep they dive to find food. They can also find out how far the sharks travel each year.

WHO'S UNDER ATTACK?

5 PEOPLE DEAD IN ONE YEAR!

Every year, sharks will attack about 60 people. They will kill just five of them.

270,000 SHARKS DEAD IN ONE DAY!

Every day, about 270,000 sharks are killed. Most are caught as food for people. Shark meat is sold in stores and restaurants. Some sharks die by accident. They are caught in fishing nets meant to catch other fish.

Every year, millions of sharks have their fins cut off. The fins are used to make shark-fin soup, which is an expensive food in some countries. The sharks are then thrown back in the water — still alive. They soon bleed to death.

SHARK ALERT
Many types of shark are now very rare. This includes great white sharks. Many shark species could soon become **extinct**.

NEED-TO-KNOW WORDS

breach When a shark jumps out of the water to grab prey

bull shark A type of shark, also known as a river whaler. This large shark is one of the few sharks that swims up rivers. Bull sharks have been seen in the Amazon River, over 1,800 miles (2,900 kilometers) from the ocean.

chainmail suit An outfit made from small metal rings connected together into chains

detect To sense or feel something

extinct When a species of animal or plant has died out and there are none left

frenzy To behave in a wild, uncontrolled way

great white shark The largest species of hunting shark

prey An animal that is hunted and eaten by another animal

pulses Short bursts of electricity

shark net Nets that stop sharks from swimming in too close to the shoreline

species A group of animals that look similar and can breed with each other

tiger shark One of the largest species of shark. The tiger shark gets its name from the stripes along its back and on its tail fin.

torpedoed To attack, strike, or sink with a torpedo

victims People or animals who are hurt or killed

NEED-TO-KNOW DATA

Largest:
Whale shark
up to 50 feet (15 meters) long

Smallest:
Dwarf lanternshark
up to 7.5 inches
(19 centimeters) long

Protecting sharks:

- Don't eat shark-fin soup or shark meat.

- Don't buy shark souvenirs, such as shark teeth and jaws.

- Don't buy belts, bags, or shoes made from shark skin.

- Don't buy herbal medicines that contain shark cartilage.

SHARKS ONLINE

http://www.discoverychannel.com.au/sharks/index.shtml
http://animals.nationalgeographic.com/animals/fish.html
http://www.bite-back.com/
http://www.gct.org/sharkmain.html

Publisher's note to educators and parents:
Our editors have carefully reviewed these websites to ensure that they are suitable for children. Many websites change frequently, however, and we cannot guarantee that a site's future contents will continue to meet our high standards of quality and educational value. Be advised that children should be closely supervised whenever they access the Internet.